Thank You for the Window Office

Maged Zaher

UDP · 2012

ISBN 978-1-933254-97-5
Distributed to the trade by
Small Press Distribution
www.spdbooks.org

First Edition, First Printing
Limited to 850 copies

Ugly Duckling Presse
The Old American Can Factory
232 Third Street #E-303
Brooklyn, NY 11215

Cover design by Lyric Hunter
Typeset by Don't Look Now! in Fournier and Caecilia

Printed and bound at McNaughton & Gunn
Covers offset-printed at Polyprint Design

Some of these poems previously appeared in 6X6, *Alice Blue Review*,
Capitalism Nature Socialism, *Filter*, *Rattapallax*, and *Saltgrass*

This book was made possible in part by a generous grant from
the National Endowment for the Arts

NATIONAL
ENDOWMENT
FOR THE ARTS

To Marcel Nasif and Pam Brown

I am hiding my vulnerability at the shawarma shop
Some people need to die for civilization's sake
Let me tell you about my exotic country then
Let me also tell you about the danger of not having a poetic project
Your dress invokes my longing for reality
I have a standard response for good looks
And the feeling that I will be punished for it
And that I will have to head back home to jerk off under pressure
The hit man is hungry
He needs encouraging text messages
Let us hear Hamlet moan because of his sore nipples
I have to stay here and ask for a better menu next war
There are people in the pub slowly eating their way into life

Being classically trained and stuff
I left this small-time success story behind
Poetry isn't about music or ideas or things
I made paper before and it hurts
Homesick and scarred—the text is shooting at our desires
(This is an approximation of course)
I was at the Marx-in-the-Park festival
They made sure we knew that there is no such thing
As perfectly parallel streets
So armed with knowledge about nutrition
We will integrate our business strategy
With God's will
Please note that people who are assertive travel a lot

So what if you just ate an overpriced burger

It is love that will eventually make a difference

And to hold the earth with one hand

You need a larger notebook

I am tired of history

I am tired of this poem

I just want to tell the same story to different people

About the dancer who brought my friend happiness

She told him about the drama of having an accent

"Do you at least love me?"—he said to his doctor

Who replied: "We have to keep the news about the project a secret

But not the loneliness of the engineers"

I am dreaming

I am dreaming that

I am dancing to a rhythm

And that I am not interested in going to the cash machine yet

Dear Poet—death is just another tool for the living to use
And soccer is a wonderful sport
Even with all the time spent driving around
Here is one more thing to sacrifice for meaning—
I am alive but I lied to you
About the random desires I keep having
(Some distortions will keep making sense)
So what if we objectify each other?
Life better be a song
That is starting soon
We are mere productions of power
At least by feeling entirely surrounded
The rest of the rest are drunk
Including the Egyptian who is waiting
We will fuck you over kindly if you cross us
The virus that swept the computer today
Is not to be taken seriously

We stood up and appealed to death

Oh! the hyper sensitivity of the small bourgeoisie

When someone asks about the mechanics of the world

And we have to answer back

Then imagine a straightforward future

While being actively anxious

I will talk to the sexy girl about immigration issues

Cover up the sins of everybody

Like a martyr

Of course I don't believe myself

Hence I look so innocent in these pictures

Power is often an approximation

You should go to New York often

To zoom up on nostalgia

Yesterday I invited a woman
To my mid-life crisis
She adjusted her scarf and asked:
"How often will you agree with me?
The fact that you don't have a tv
Will help me interpret your dreams"
I replied: "My friends are on their way to Europe
In search of good kissers
And I am living with the hope that somewhere a woman
Will undo an extra button of her shirt"

In the helicopter important people are doing important things
They are—for example—singing
And carrying important patients to hospitals
We are all walking the city streets without a chance of sex
The skinny bartender had this kind look
As if to say: "You need to look mysterious
Otherwise you will endanger the whole plan"
Even terrorists need some love
And you have something to learn about my feelings
I will start by putting you on a pedestal
Then talk to some political representative
Who will remind us of the importance of positioning
I will mention the tears that hit me in airports or in Cairo's streets
It is time to exchange one exile for another

Gravity arrived in a cab

Meanwhile three different treasure hunts were going on downtown

Please forgive our group their racial composition, Your Honor

The translator is thinking of the bodies of strangers

In my memory I located the texture of the theatre seat

You were sitting next to me

In my memory there is also a short order cook taking a nap,

A Marxist scholar studying utopia,

And a hostess who is tired

Outside of my memory there is a mortgage broker

And three environmental activists having breakfast

You look at your phone as if it matters

And scream three times before you inform them of your loneliness

You tell me: "Five more minutes to reach intimacy"

My mind is full of sexual images

Of many young academics arriving at the conference

With their hostile lovers

I ate my leftovers yesterday

Today I am planning

To start a new poem

I want to write the jaywalker's aesthetics manifesto:
Love seems like some sort of violence
So while crossing the street toward a Subway shop
There is often a group of ideas to balance in your head
This was the time when urine was often mixed with blood
Language was what made it all happen
When things didn't go my way then I never threw a fit
I just jumped from boats mid-distance to shore in order to impress myself
Or defended my favorite musician and kissed him on the forehead
Then analyzed the cartographer's intention
To end the world with his prayers
We understood capitalism then
Or what it looked like under the pressure of alcohol

The city was loaded with small-time investment bankers
And the occasional sexual tourists
(Our main business is obedience to people with important illusions)
My visit was thought of as a political move
Now I can say things like: "She is the one who started the kinky sex lesson"
You are the driver
And we managed to go around the world during a thousand rush hours
The young woman took his insanity seriously
She asked: "Can you stay around after tennis?"
And because I abstracted everything: the Danish
Women at the party, the sidewalks of the ghetto, etc.
I am sending three cheers to the poets of Cairo
And their longing for good vodka

He thought that the Dalai Lama was a nice guy with important things to say
Yet deep down Marx was still his rock star
The whole effort was a waste—especially thinking
About the Udhri poets' re-enactment of the crime scene of love
Meanwhile I told them that it didn't hurt as much anymore
It was just the right time to sleep
Two weeks later we started the no-shoes campaign
And disappeared precisely when expected
Get some alcohol, son
Mix it with coffee and think about
The number of real estate sales in California
I am using my symptoms effectively
But I won't be approving of them anytime soon

This is a badly decorated crisis—
Time to migrate to the next condo
All lines of poetry are created equal
So deliver your speech without background music
I finished my dream
Then with a skateboarder's single mindedness
I went to the market
Some porn is taken for granted
Hopefully you can see
This poem is struggling hard
To be on someone's top ten list
You always said: "Capitalism made me do it"
It is sometimes irrational to be irrational
And whatever you wear on Casual Fridays is up to you
Or so said the cockroaches of hope
For a dollar you can have a glimpse at the Dalai Lama's soul
I need this poem to make it to the playoffs tomorrow

While thinking about your lips
He also thought about the pick-up algorithm
Later he told me: "I am not rigorous enough"
He also said: "I got my friends the books
They needed, yet nothing changed"
Poverty is not well-hidden
We follow the same timetable
Except that I am not falling in love tonight
The imagination always kicks reality's ass
So let's step out for a cigarette or two
On our way we can visit the media lab
And learn about the organization of dreams
We are surrounded by different kinds of sale items
We need to ask for their forgiveness
Then leave for the craft store to flirt with the experts

Hello roller coaster
Hello soup du jour precious feelings
Here we do sales
There they do shopping
In the resurrection's parade
I took a different name
Which was an inevitable twist to the plot
Yet someone in the organization had to ask:
"Is people management an essential skill?"
The bohemian is still alive

Take a number my dear friend
These are the leaders of the industry
They go to the Skywalker Ranch to discuss stuff
And these are the masses—they buy the stuff the leaders create
Now I will teach you the best cock block move I know
Because it is time to save civilization
One iPhone user at a time
Historical materialists of Cairo unite
And let us partake in the power of the masses
I saw the great minds of my generation working
For Microsoft and Boeing to be laid off later
Like dogs
I am a descendant of those who drank themselves to death
And I am glad to report—there are so many red Cadillacs at the lodge

Someone said: "mass suicide can be erotic"
So was Chairman Mao's cultural revolution
Okay—let's flirt again:
    One plane, one shuttle,
        Four metro lines, and here you are—
            An occasional muse
But you give Rasta men a bad name
And you don't have the right to sleep
I am preparing an erratic dance
To please the board of directors
Dear random coworker
Since the whole point is to have a fetish
Can you imagine what some S&M would do to this poem?
I will concede that she is wearing a nice hijab
And that I understand poetry to be about both fucking
And fucking up

Farmers marry farmers
This was a childhood lesson
The text is more profound before it is written
I am in a Cairo coffee shop recording facts
Don't let your occasional fuck buddy dictate the orgasm situation
The world has changed and I misplaced the email
Every human-to-human touch carries a probability
Otherwise where to go when we turn around and sleep
There are no sexual activities at the gym
The trainers now fuck on their own time
But people here are concerned with justice
They are important and kind

Love in the frozen vegetables aisle
Lap-dance security forces
Why do you care about the well being of the enemy?
I am wondering—how could anyone trust anyone
Writing a collection of Star Wars poems?
She was the go-go dancer from hell
He was a poet fond of clichés
Eventually an infinite amount of sadness
Accumulated in the IT department
Heidegger Hegel Wittgenstein Kant
Spinoza Kierkegaard Nietzsche
Transcendentalists Empiricists
Benjamin Adorno Marx Situationist International
Foucault Habermas Derrida Žižek
Deleuze Deleuze and Guattari
Edward Said Fred Jameson Terry Eagleton

I will give you this: There is a conceptual gap in some love stories
You whisper to me about the oddities of software
I hover over the loneliness embedded in the act of making a choice
And we read manifestoes to each other
Working software is the primary way of showing progress
Let me think of myself politically for a moment
Having a high sex drive is an emotional hurdle
You have to learn the trick
I have to learn the trick
Because it is often sad to touch the pages of the books I will never read
I am working my way toward the Q&A session
I am looking at the machine and the love it provides
And doing some reaching out because my feelings are hurt

Floods happen
And political assassinations too
But the ones who stayed cashed in big
A mysterious sound spoke slowly:
"Did you introduce yourself to your city yet?"
The Udhri poets were playing peek-a-boo with their desert muses
I am more into watching soccer in a British pub
Next to a woman eating fish and chips
(I know that I have to think of her romantically)
The bartender is reading his second manifesto
The Udhri poets were not big into fucking
Which understandably disappointed their muses
"Power concedes nothing"—my friend announced
I said: "We will be outsourced soon
Let us just reach out into someone's impossible life
And make the sign of the cross"
I am still expected to solve important business problems
Cairo, I miss walking your streets before dawn:

 My body—a disclaimer

 And you—a random metaphor

Splitting a cardamom pod in two is a violent act
Now that I am threatened by everything
I can say the truth:
The staff is pierced and shy
I am looking for ways to work remotely
And be radical about it
This is how accidents work:
   Fitting one poem at a time
   Into a mid-sized cab
   Without disturbing the poetics
   Of the passing cars

In this poem there is a man and a woman
They are dancing
One is ambivalent
And one is reading Marx and thinking:
"I created a space for my body to feel inadequate"
The whole story is of course tragic
With a comic touch
But we are in the middle of a presidential race
And stale love is a matter of national security
I am reaching this form on my own
But I worry if I say the right things to authority figures
And if a U-turn in this busy street
Is all I need for now

The things we took for granted—
    The kids who beat us periodically
    And the metaphors we used for bragging—
Didn't cause much disappointment
It was hope that really screwed us
Riding in the same trolley
During the short business hours
And being occasionally hurt
By fashion and other things
We hang out in the camel area
To pick-up tourists
And I feel my cell phone's vibrations
Asking the big questions of the universe
One more poet stepping into nihilism
Sitting at the Cosmopolitan—downtown Cairo
All big questions have one good answer—
Here—downtown Cairo—poets take alcohol seriously
I am more concerned about my desires
And how to articulate them often

Poetry is a ghost

That erases the good news

If you believe in friendship at first sight

Then spank me

It is my birthday

And I've already found a gap in the world—

    Ask me not to panic

    Because these words can be taken seriously

The aliens were jet-lagged
Having one eye and fifty hands didn't help
The poem is a division of labor
Occasionally the muse gets pissed off
If you lose her purse
The others were grinding their teeth
The corporation approved us and advised: step up
We were just drunk not angry
And wondering about all the people
Who can't expense their dinners
Then God—on a bad day—invented the poets

On Friday the corporate printer bin is full of coupons
Direct presence of the world is impossible
My friend always has a crush on the wrong woman
This poem can be assumed to be hetero-normative
I just love the idea of adventure
Like being in an earthquake and discussing lust
All these days at the gym—macho yet romantic
I am working hard to accumulate money

Leading the world again
Toward a solid business model
Digital pork chops for everyone
All the street signs are suddenly in English
I have to wake up, then do something difficult
Like letting go of five friends, then whispering
Did your faith help you today?
The cook was stranded on the island
The polite dragons came to say goodbye
Or check out the drama teacher's body

You are a free spirit
With a good hugging pose
I need editors with extravagant fetishes
To have conversations about wine
The Greyhound is an appropriate observation deck
How often do you have a legitimate reason
To erase the neighborhood from your memory?
We asked the candidate: "Are you a team player?
And if so, what do you want for breakfast?"
Don't bring the executioner home
Surprisingly I still make sense
No matter how redundant the text
Gravity will always stick around

There are different kinds of pills to take in hotels
Line up all the candles
No more superheroes
Love might cover up bad logistics
But your arms are getting older than you are
Only few stories remain
Of men who are the pride of their towns
And the women who loved them
Line up all the candles
One nation under the sea

Don't assume lots of roles in one life
Infinity grows bigger over time
I've reached the age where I am asked for reference
And receive lazy threats about Viagra
You are on display 100% of the time
Change your shape according to the law
Occasionally you can sneak in an entrepreneurial move
Then leave to check on your kids
Not all of us in the porn industry are sexy
I will disclose my age in a few milliseconds

Given all the lab tests they ran
I am not thirsty or useful
Lust is fleeting
Even with a sexy accent
You are allowed two pieces of luggage
Because it is cold at destination
The millionaire's text is everywhere—
Welcome to averagehood everyone
Stratification pays off
I am sure the DVDs will be collected
Before the end of the flight

A world of coupons
In the dangerous part of the city
The imagination fails one sentence at a time
Should have stayed home
Instead of letting poetry make it impossible to drive
Write your narrative here
We all need soft drinks
The poet insists on kissing strangers
Maybe one would give birth to a beautiful frog
This is a war we need to win on merits
The jukebox is playing French music
And now you have to answer the same question twice
Don't forget your jacket in straight bars

Would you believe me
If I shaved the protagonist's head
And claimed we can walk the streets defeated?
Would you still have the same crush on him?
Ah, the anguish of robots when they run out of electricity
Knifed in the alley
All the subplots are coming together
A loaf of bread for dinner
We never understood the intentions of the stabbed or the stabber
There was a voicemail when we got home
And enough material to build a small ninja-training camp

Take your memories to the kitchen
Where they can't block you from talking to your children
This is a rare moment when your student loans bring you joy
Yet pleasure is prohibited tonight
I said: "Let's be good technologists"
There is enough room for all interpretations
And I have to email you again about my feelings
I need two water-cooler conversations a day
I will write you a letter about breathing
And about the left-over glue the brochure makers keep leaving behind

Mute the sound, and watch the images follow each other
I want to do more shameful things tonight
Like playing the famous angels against each other
Or having a green card marriage
There were people in bright orange vests in the streets
The homeland is secure today except from my thoughts:
The easiest way to make friends is to sleep with them
The EU is full of good croissants
Desire is expensive
And my generic loneliness is overdue

It is useless to remind you of my flaws
For example I am an outsider by choice
Which—as you know—makes me
Hopelessly middle class

I am here to report back
The exploration of my subconscious was fruitful
How often should you open the refrigerator door
In order to watch
The structure of habits form?
We can imagine being the soccer fanatics
Who stayed soccer fanatics
Despite the changes to the rules
I attached my desires to this email
Please review them carefully

Watching from the airport tower
Some guy called for the cook
"You should have thought of greatness as an exit plan"
Alcohol bottles flying
Let me suggest some ad-hoc therapy
The experience will fill you with joy
Please be seated
And save your questions for God until the end of the seminar
You should expect miracles though
After a long session of assertive prayers

The moon is there for everyone
Seven days without poetry
I am surrounded by process improvement diagrams
A good fate for an ascetic
To always be making business decisions
In Sunday school I learned: Think of the angels as hip DJs
Who line up treasures for us
I asked too many questions
And damaged all the gift-wrapping
It wasn't just an identity issue
Believe me—we had to develop the weapon
The dragon ate the fish and there was no lunch left

Choose one specific room to hang the posters
Romanticism was something to brag about
Tonight we have a meeting with the absolute
As imagined by a magician
Once again I am surrounded by people with big visions
The bride, however, is falling for the photographer
And the paper airplanes flying nearby
They added one number to the area code
The world was one continuous tabloid article
Peer pressure to walk on tables
Courage is a bad toothpaste brand opportunity
One more interview with a successful CEO
One more poem about police brutality
Thank you for the opportunity to join the subculture

One drama per night is enough for this small stage

The outsider is caving in, hoping for a better exchange rate

As anxiety builds minute-by-minute

They are closing tabs all over town

The bartenders asked all the right questions

And we planned against the anticipated pain

The phone rang in meeting room number three

We received the signal

To start Operation Fend off the Mystics

The realists were also evacuated

And the old homegrown music was back again

All the bell captains were equally surprised

Because of the new set of smooth pick-up lines

And we were turned away from the spaceship

The flight attendant whispered to me: "Did you think

You would die if I loved you back?"

This is the pre-season
Intellectuals are sought after
There are cubicle walls to be moved
And there is also this woman who wants to kiss me
The sidewalk is becoming more metaphysical everyday
Actually the whole city now is discussing Hegel
It is soothing though to remember your customer number
Because of all the rich technologists sitting at the bar
My only friend in town—the one who died twice before—is away
So I have to act like a good repairman
Who is into espionage and the occult
Or like an ancient Arab poet near the remains of his departed tribe
Having tangential thoughts of sand, tents, and a whole community of ants

What is a city without its interpretation
Without a dance club where straights kiss
Without street cars
Without the risk of being wiped out by a tornado or an earthquake
Come visit us soon
We will experience major cuts
And the boys who hang out here will die
Until you are back
Carrying with you the complexity of money
Everything feels strange
The streets of the old city
And the heaven everyone dreams of

This is an imaginary city
It has seven hills
And is always ready for your software needs
I will describe it gracefully
But first let me tell you about my mysterious encounter with magic
The street beggars are walking
Old people too
They extract the nightness of the night
These are good ducks in the park
Now—what to do with the thought that people lived
And died miserably?
And that all the religious and Marxist books
Can't change anything about that?

A comfortable chair for the poem
I am not worried—but then, I need more wisdom
Can you instead get me a heated croissant?
Revolutions need people with good hair
Lenin, Subcommandante Marcos, Chavez...
Ok—so reality is a little confusing
Justice will remain a simple data point
Language is always good to express the middle class
Money and roses for everyone else

Don't sell your season tickets
Enough annoying kids are going into finance
The first pitch is a good indicator
Because our suffering is physical
For example: allergies, lay-offs, and crucifixions
I admit I am not associated with anybody
Which is inevitably a radical move
Yet I am one of the poets who cry
In the company of other poets
Is it possible to consult Heidegger's love letters
About the next steps?
All my friends are alive
I have no record this poem ever happened
The beautiful girls all went to marketing

In Reykjavik now some people are dancing
They filmed the Golden Gate Bridge when she was walking
Alright—this is supposed to be serious
I am stuck with pain in my fingers
The intellectuals are buying cheap goods
My basic fear is keeping the systems in sync
Of course this longing is sexual
Although I like this nonsense about sublimating desire
We can still assume everything is separate from everything else
Welcome to Amsterdam Central Station

People eventually stop sending you party reminders
And schedules empty out
With few poems to rescue
No one cares about the flag
But some anarchists are also patriotic
I am asking to be kindly left out
They have lots of rugs downtown
They are on perpetual sale
But they help us fight back the communists

Now that we have touch-screen notebooks
Some proximity to the water will suffice
But whom do you talk to for inspiration?
Suddenly, a certain metaphor feels inadequate
Lots of Dutch people in Amsterdam
All the middle class turned into bad tourists
Okay—so you don't want to be my mistress
Only my spiritual guide?
The poem is a gift—like semen
Or like beer
In the morning I smell of hotel soap
Naturally there is time to stop and think
And time for auditors to ask the tough questions

You are the king but you are angry
There is wisdom in accumulating goods
Especially the goods sold at high margin
One barista—infinite orders
Which is a threat that will last for a while
Time to start your own commerce activities
We are experiencing longing
And a little bit of hurt
I will arrange for you to be someone else
When I start using my powerful time machine
While in business we will always love each other

The poem will end

Okay—I didn't mean to be that melodramatic

I mean there are always road accidents

They won't leave the dance floor tonight

Even if I start reading Das Capital out loud

So there is love—and it collapses

Under the mercy of production

You stood there—angry and fragile

Out of childhood fear

And the Marxists' failures

Which is almost the saddest thing you know

Time to sit here and feel inadequate

The promoters killed the party

It is not patriotic to accept the kisses of a stranger

Here is a space to be sane

Now keep the volume down

And stick to sadness

Even with such generous sweet potato portions

The DJ realized he needed to accept requests

We are to pretend that all competitors are created equal

The poet at the soccer game
Reciting from Homer's Twitter feed
Tires everywhere
Piles of used Xboxes
The bearded folks surrounding the entrance
One of us will get to be the boss
And feel the joys of the class system
One will die of fear
And although the guru said nothing about jerking off
I will manage to wear green
And offend no one today

This poem brings up love in a clichéd fashion
We argued a lot with the freedom fighters
And I promised them a couple of orgasms
The city looked okay from the window
But if you clicked on the zoom button
You would find a homeless man
Who is totally forgotten
He brings his loneliness everywhere
He also brings his desires
And asks someone about aesthetics

Male strippers also get their feelings hurt
Despite your theoretical efforts you will stay skinny
There are times to be ruthless
For example when axing expensive labor
There are problems that can only be solved when alive
In the middle of the acquisition meeting
I thought of Frank O'Hara walking New York streets
My lunch poems were composed over Chinese take out
While we decided whom to fire
There are standard gestures in this world
Like my buying you a drink
Despite the obvious fact
That infinite people are infinitely poor

Let us be accurate:
Are you calling me in the middle of the night
To talk about philosophy or about aesthetics?
I am somehow mad at everything
But this time I will earn my place on public transportation
I swallow a couple of words every day
Then knock on my neighbor's door
To ask him to stop using these words for a week
I learned the hard way
That it is important to eat lettuce when rooting for democracy
But if you are growing up poor and angry
Then you need to understand the billboard messages

Occasionally at a crammed coffee shop
I discover some profound truth
For example: An insanely handsome celebrity lives nearby
Or that God sometimes protects the middle class
Sadness always arrives later
While reading a poem by a poet who just died
Graduate school proves useless
There are always bootstrapping problems
And people who uphold the law
And circus clowns who are not liable for damages

On why I became a terrorist:
My childhood was bad—
The government invited everyone to brunch
But showed up late
Having a sexy mother didn't help either
So I composed poems
While watching you drink
There is suffering in the universe
It can give you pleasant feelings to know
That others are also tired
The futurists were on our backs
Never agree to the fifteen-minute rule

I am rearranging the letters
On the tv stand
In order to make sense
Of my own flesh
Never expected
That cultural experiences
Could end that badly
My syntax will work
And yes—your age, your dress
And the visibility of my dreadlocks
Are all poetry material
It is ugly though
To oppose the commandments
Even if in the high court
They secretly have erotic thoughts
About animals

You are cute—I am cute

It is even

The cubists in their cubes are waiting

For someone to invent the cheeseburger

The data is categorized

And squeezed into the brains

Of a few lucky employees

We call this management

It stands and watches the poet read

A poem about a big gas station

It is called

The Big Gas Station Poem

In Paris I heard

They have umbrellas

And they have croissants

I also heard that

Spirituality helps on the job

And that when you are ready

We will disappear together

Suddenly I am interested in local politics
How much immunization should we provide for free?
I am in the airport and I need to write an airport poem
Being from Cairo do you still like Elvis?
Maria is writing her second book as we speak
Being martyrs my colleagues abandoned hope
In finding the appropriate software
They walk the hallways with shaved heads and visible genitals
The private sector had to step in and save the day

There were hipsters before the hipsters
That you think of as hipsters existed
And there is nothing wrong with that—
It is just a timing issue
You need to fight hard
For the Space Needle
Because militants are beautiful creatures
So are the sexy ferries
We live in a subset of the universe
Made out of three people
Inside this subset we are scared
Of being excluded from sales promotions

The information society crept up on us
But now—armed with new ways of looking at things—
We make coffee daily
Do you know how tiring the business of revolution is?
I will analyze someone's Madonna-whore complex
It all started with an argument about religion
Then—inspired by tv ads—the fantasy continued
So as not to make more mistakes than I have to
I will craft sentences out of the permutations
Of imaginary alphabets
In the USA—Mexicans cook for everyone
I know you were oppressed as a child and as an engineer
However it is time to ask the priestess to leave
There is a heavy political component to all this twitching

Sometimes we fail to communicate
And it is lots of fun
(As if there is glitter everywhere)
But thank you for the poem

Sleeping with the beautiful woman
Doesn't really matter
Because on a trip elsewhere
I won't count the syllables
And the poem will act angry
Which is a half-assed tragedy
The longing is disruptive though
And having a new intelligence director
Is an opportunity for joy
Few bookstores are open today
And I have this love for humanity except you

This is where famous spies used to hang out

Good breathing is utilized by good detectives

Do you remember sleeping in the same bed?

Day in, day out—I am feeling sad

Can you talk to someone important about this?

I am writing my memoir

About selling the house for the angry lovers

Keeping the receipts won't help

You have to fire people every now and then

Waking up tomorrow—the world will hurt less

Actually I am lying

I am always lying

Give me a refillable pen
And I will build you an illusion
Do you understand how most machines work?
Typically you feed them humans
Or you wait until the poem
Stops sounding like anything you know
How many happy hours do you need to experience
Before you stop singing along?
We will party hard tomorrow
With the sales executives
For now let's just talk about our musical preferences

They selected me to die
I am proud though of the design I left on the whiteboard
And as I am close enough to heaven
It is time to remove this sentence

I won't die in Paris on a rainy day
I will be building technological platforms
And the business architects
Will be in perfect agreement with me
(The official design strategy will annoy all of us)
And I will nap for thirty minutes
Then die

A good San Francisco investment banker
Will offer you a job
In exchange for bad sex
Thank you for the pain
I will stop manipulating you
And I will have an abortion
Then lick between your open legs
For a full night

I have a pub life
Where pages about science
Disappear or get erased by strong governments
I also go to watch my friends
Die doing their homework
I am still ecstatic though about someone winning the World Cup
Because my friends will stay behind
To guard the poetics for everyone
Then draw lots of diagrams about the business process
And all the beautiful women watching soccer
In this pub where I have a life
Old tourists jerk off in the bathroom
Youth brings a sense of despair
There are different ways to drag ourselves behind
Lots of assumptions behind managing your friends

Some days metaphors just don't cut it
The home team is on the road
And I am in love with a blonde bike messenger
I am pouring tea in my cup on my lap
The city is overbuilt
And cars make unnecessary U-turns
This poem is not working
Because an old map is still available
In the well-lit corners of the castle

Monsters have a different value system
They stare at blue lines
And sell media to everyone
Bikes are here to stay
Some agitation is needed
Because some poems are deeply Maoist
Mistrust goes a long way
I need to list all the patents we hold
Give me value or give me death

This is a poem for the IT martyrs:
The ocean doesn't save its creatures
The airport doesn't either
Okay—how to survive without a keyboard?
I lost my cold glass:
    Denial, anger, depression, acceptance
To ask a question or not to ask a question
Ending up in a mass grave
This poem is my last kiss to the happy hour crowd
I am angry
But I am going to lunch
I am going to lunch and need your blessing

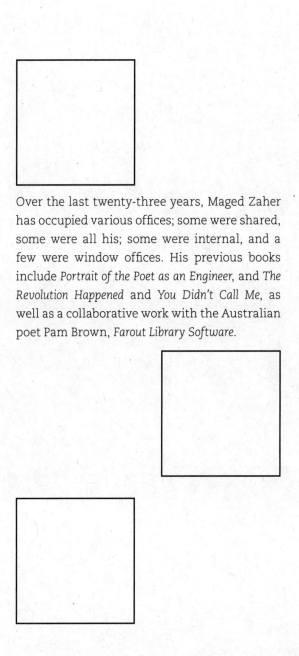

Over the last twenty-three years, Maged Zaher has occupied various offices; some were shared, some were all his; some were internal, and a few were window offices. His previous books include *Portrait of the Poet as an Engineer*, and *The Revolution Happened* and *You Didn't Call Me*, as well as a collaborative work with the Australian poet Pam Brown, *Farout Library Software*.

Recent poetry titles from Ugly Duckling Presse

For a complete catalog please see our website:
www.uglyducklingpresse.org

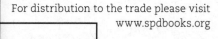

For distribution to the trade please visit
www.spdbooks.org